MENTAL MOTIVATION

Presented to...

May this book bless you in your spirit, soul, and mind. Thank you for the support.

To contact the author:

@RobLWattsJr

drrlwjr@gmail.com

*We are what we repeatedly do. Excellence, therefore, is not an act but a habit ~ **Aristotle***

40 Empowerment Thoughts

Acknowledgements...

I want to give a special acknowledgement to my purpose driven wife, Natalie, and precious daughter, Trinity; thank you both for being the gems that you are to me. My two inspirations to push, press, pursue, and persevere.

A special thanks to the Younique Design, Inc. publishing team, for your tireless efforts. I greatly appreciate the contributing editors, Juanita Shaffer, *MA*, Janet Anthony, *PhD*, and Tamike Hurley, *MA*, for assisting me in effectively articulating the message. Thanks to our church family and ministry partners, being able to serve you and serve with you keeps me sharpened.

Thank you to my family and friends, who are always there to support what God is doing through the Watts Trio.

Drs. Eugene and Andrea Mason, you've been asking for the booklet, so here it is! Your continuous support is tremendously appreciated.

MENTAL MOTIVATION
40 Empowerment Thoughts

Robert L. Watts, Jr.

40 Empowerment Thoughts

MENTAL MOTIVATION:
40 Empowerment Thoughts
Copyright © 2015 by Robert L. Watts, Jr.

Published by
Younique Design, Inc.
Illinois
www.youniquedesign.biz/menu

Unless otherwise indicated, all Scripture quotations are taken from the New King James and King James Version of the Bible. Unless otherwise indicated, all definition quotations are taken from web source, **www.dictionary.com**. February 2015

Library of Congress Control Number: 2014955028

All rights reserved. This book or any portion thereof may not be reproduced or used in any manner whatsoever without the express written permission of the author. The views expressed in this book are not necessarily those of the publisher.

Printed in the United States of America
First Printing, 2015
ISBN 978-0-9831339-3-3

MENTAL MOTIVATION

Literary Forgiveness...

Should there be a grammatical oversight found, we respectfully ask that you don't allow a grammatical error or a preferred writing style block you from the message that God wants you to receive. Enjoy!

~~~~~~~~~~~~~~~~~~~~~~~~~~~~~~

"If the world was perfect, it wouldn't be."
~Yogi Berra

"If you're not making mistakes, then you're not doing anything..."
~John Wooden

"Not that I have already obtained all this, or have already been made perfect, but I press on to take hold of that which Christ Jesus took hold of me."
~Philippians 3:12 (NIV)

40 Empowerment Thoughts

~1~

To obtain *favor* with *flavor*, seek the heart of God.

The LORD said to Moses, "I will also do this thing of which you have spoken; for you have found favor in My sight and I have known you by name."
***Exodus** 33:17*

MENTAL MOTIVATION

Nothing is comparable to obtaining God's favor. It is where the impossible becomes possible. God instructed Moses to lead the Israelites out of Egypt into the Promised Land. Due to this life assignment, Moses needed much strength and guidance, so he communed with God regularly. Moses found favor with God to the point they could converse as friends! (Read Exodus 33:11-14, which enlightens us with insight on obtaining and sustaining the kind of favor with flavor Moses experienced.)

When God adds *flavor* to His *favor*, He will make it known that His hand is supernaturally on you. Not only will God restore, but He'll give you more. The Israelites experienced this through the extraordinary miracles, such as: the parting of the Red Sea and manna falling from Heaven. Seeking the heart of God is a key ingredient to obtaining that level of favor in your life.

THOUGHTS TO ACTION...
- ➤ Ask God to teach you His ways.
- ➤ Practice pursuing what pleases God.
- ➤ Use the knowledge learned about God to grow in intimacy with Him.
- ➤ Stand on the promises that God gave to you and remind Him of them.

~2~

Don't let your reality blur the truth of the matter.

For we walk by faith, not by sight.
2 Corinthians 5:7

MENTAL MOTIVATION

Believers in Christ are supposed to walk by faith and not by sight, but we are bound by this doubting flesh! In the midst of troubled situations, we can easily become distracted by what is before our eyes in the natural. Our human reality can often trump and react in the flesh, if it isn't disciplined to filter life's situations through our faith.

Faith lenses reveal the 'truth' of the matter, but our human vision is restricted to the facts of the situation. The Word reminds us to renew our minds (Romans 12:2) for our thoughts are the core of us (Proverbs 23:7). The flesh and spirit are always at war; the one you feed the most will be the strongest. Exercise the faith lenses to develop keen perception to avoid deception.

THOUGHTS TO ACTION…
- ➢ Refresh your mind with the Word of God and with other faith resources.
- ➢ Speak to your situation in faith with The Word according to God's Will.
- ➢ Believe that it shall come to pass.
- ➢ Rejoice as if your reality has already changed.

~3~
Don't forget to *pray*, otherwise you become *prey*.

Continue in prayer, and watch in the same with thanksgiving;
Colossians 4:2

MENTAL MOTIVATION

Prey is defined as, *one that is defenseless, especially in the face of attack; a victim*. This is exactly what we become when we do not practice *kneeology*: on our knees in continual prayer. 1 Peter 5:8 warns us that the devil is on a prowl looking for whom to consume destructively.

Prayer positions us in a good offensive posture, prepared to be a victor and not a victim. Practicing daily prayer increases our intimacy with God, which is where the enemy's secrets are exposed, and the Holy Spirit reveals the strategy to overcome.

THOUGHTS TO ACTION...

- Make prayer a lifestyle (intentional discipline) and not a mechanical habit.
- Read the scripture daily so you know and understand TRUTH.
- Continually ask God for wisdom and insight in all situations.
- Target your prayers not against flesh and blood, but towards the evil in the spirit realm that is out to steal, kill, and destroy (Ephesian 6:12).

40 Empowerment Thoughts

~4~
Your *Perspective* determines Your *Focus.*

Finally, brethren, whatsoever things are true, whatsoever things are honest, whatsoever things are just, whatsoever things are pure, whatsoever things are lovely, whatsoever things are of good report; if there be any virtue, and if there be any praise, think on these things.
Philippians 4:8

MENTAL MOTIVATION

If we were to put four people in different areas of a room and ask them to describe the same object in the room, there would be four various descriptions of the same object. The reason is they are all at different positions in the room.

Perspective is how a person sees things based on his or her point-of-view. Our perspectives are shaped by our upbringing, education, experiences, personality temperaments, and life influencers. Be conscious of the fact, that what you are *focused* on is based on your 'perspective filters' and it may not be the whole picture of a situation. We must discipline our view through God's eyes. Seek out all facts and other perspectives before making final decisions and/or conclusions.

THOUGHTS TO ACTION...
- ➢ Be open and embrace change.
- ➢ Surround yourself with others who are different from you but have similar goals.
- ➢ Seek understanding of the situations.
- ➢ Empower yourself through educational tools to broaden your perspective.

~5~
Your *Approach* determines Your *Outcome*.

We demolish arguments and every pretension that sets itself up against the knowledge of God, and we take captive every thought to make it obedient to Christ.
2 Corinthians 10:5(NIV)

MENTAL MOTIVATION

How do you deal with situations? Do you quickly react? Do you take your time to ponder before responding? Or do you tend to ignore the situation? However, you go about dealing with a situation, it is important to first consider your desired result. You must stop, pray, and think before executing any actions.

Our circle of influence, thought process, personality temperament, experiences, child-rearing, and core values are the ingredients that result in our methods of approach. We must continue to cultivate our response mechanisms to ensure the maximized life available to us, in all areas of our lives. We do not have to settle for mediocrity; and be sure to make your approaches intentional.

THOUGHTS TO ACTION…
- Keep the intended result in mind.
- Keep in mind the audience with whom you are dealing.
- Keep in mind of your natural reactions.
- Keep prayer in the forefront, not an after-thought.

40 Empowerment Thoughts

~6~

God is interested in your *Produce* more than your *Product*.

His lord said unto him, well done, thou good and faithful servant: thou hast been faithful over a few things, I will make thee ruler over many things: enter thou into the joy of thy lord.
Matthew 25:21

MENTAL MOTIVATION

Produce:
to bring into existence; give rise to; cause
Product:
the totality of goods or services that a company makes available; output

One of my frequent quotes is '*God is not impressed with your gift(s), because he gave it to you.*' God is more moved by our stewardship of the *gift(s)* to bring about Kingdom increase.

Notice the part in the scripture, "*thou hast been faithful over a few things...,*" indicates that the person was entrusted with his lord's possession or product. But it was his faithfulness over his lord's things that brought into existence more than what he was entrusted. God expects KROI (Kingdom Return on Investment). Each of us has been given gifts/talents for a purpose and we should not allow them to lie dormant. So let's get to producing!

THOUGHTS TO ACTION...
- Do not accept complacency.
- Never allow yourself to become arrogant about your gifts/talents.
- Cultivate your soil to be rich and fertile.
- Remember we are only stewards; God is the source.

40 Empowerment Thoughts

> ~7~
>
> **Great leaders do not cheat and compete; they lead and sow seed.**

44 And whosoever of you will be the chiefest, shall be servant of all. 45 For even the Son of Man came not to be ministered unto, but to minister, and to give his life a ransom for many.
Mark 10:44-45

MENTAL MOTIVATION

Healthy competition is good when structured to build the productivity of a team. When a leader is insecure and operates out of fear, the leadership will result in manipulation and control, in order to stay on top. A great leader's mindset should always be to look for those they can impart into in an effort to prepare the individuals to carry on the legacy of leadership in their own capacity.

Only one person has your fingerprints; YOU! Your purpose and assignment are yours. There is no need to strive to outdo anyone. Be confident that you are a leader in your own right; and as a leader you have to go before others to show *the way*. What *the way* means to each individual will vary based on their own purpose in life. Be intentional to impart wisdom and direction into those you have influence over and connect to the leader within them.

THOUGHTS TO ACTION...
- Be confident in your leadership.
- Look to cultivate others to continue the legacy of leadership and release people in love.
- Always lead in humility.
- Identify and connect with the target audience in your sphere of influence.

40 Empowerment Thoughts

~8~
Your life develops meaning when you help bring meaning to others.

Let each of you look not only to his own interests, but also to the interests of others.
Philippians 2:4 (NIV)

MENTAL MOTIVATION

Jesus is, was, and forever will be the epitome of a life with meaning. I want to use the life altering experience the Samaritan woman had with Jesus in the fourth chapter of John as an example. This Samaritan woman was living her life as she was accustomed to living. While living in her comfort zone and routine of familiarity, God, in his grace and mercy, interrupted and introduced her to *true living* through Jesus' willingness to converse with her. He did not just speak with her; he spoke LIFE into her situation rather than condemning her. As a result, her life was altered on the path of PURPOSE.

We will find that our willingness to engage with others in a meaningful way will cultivate us as we help cultivate others. Do not miss an opportunity for growth. Engage!

THOUGHTS TO ACTION…
- Don't ignore that unction when you're compelled to engage with another.
- Know that you have something to offer.
- Seek to connect with the individual versus reacting to what you see.
- Be obedient. Remember, it will not always be comfortable or convenient.

~9~

Don't let your *hang-ups hinder* you from *helping* others.

¹⁴ What good is it, my brothers and sisters, if someone claims to have faith but has no deeds? Can such faith save them? ¹⁵ Suppose a brother or a sister is without clothes and daily food. ¹⁶ If one of you says to them, "Go in peace; keep warm and well fed," but does nothing about their physical needs, what good is it?
James 2:14-16 (NIV)

MENTAL MOTIVATION

Have you experienced times when you wouldn't extend yourself to lend a helping hand, because of personal issues with the individual or your own insecurities and reservations? Most, if not all, have experienced this decision.

God has an expectation of us to help meet the needs of other people spiritually, emotionally, intellectually, financially, and physically, where applicable, based on the capacity He has given and directed us to do. Many of us have been guilty of similar responses noted in the scripture reference; using the spiritual jargon: "I'll pray for you..." and nothing more is done. I'm not charging you to put a Super "S" on your chest and save the world. It's a charge not to settle by giving ourselves an *out* in helping others, due to our own self-centered justifiable excuses.

THOUGHTS TO ACTION...
- When opportunities to help others are present, ask God for wisdom.
- Be willing to set aside your convenience if you are supposed to help.
- Realize that you are doing Kingdom sowing.
- Give the gift of empathy with those you are helping.

~10~
In conversations, avoid *'debate'* and practice to *'relate.'*

19 So then, my beloved brethren, let every man be swift to hear, slow to speak, slow to wrath; 20 for the wrath of man does not produce the righteousness of God.
James 1:19-20

MENTAL MOTIVATION

Conversations with someone who is always ready for rebuttal with statements such as, "yeah, but" or "I disagree with that", can be referred to as a *Communication Narcissist*. *This communicator* is only interested in hearing his/her own point of view and is always ready to prove the other person wrong.

Communication Narcissists don't experience the fullness of the knowledge available to them and remain in darkness and unnecessary ignorance. This form of communication causes frustration, agitation, and a disconnect with others. We must make the choice to avoid the path to unnecessary ignorance, seek truth, and experience necessary growth.

THOUGHTS TO ACTION...

- Listen twice as much as you speak; you have two ears and one mouth.
- Actively listen versus just hearing the person speaking.
- Use add-on statements like, *'here's another perspective to consider.'*
- Genuinely consider another's point of view.

~11~
Don't fall for Satan's *bait* while you *wait* on God.

Lest Satan should get an advantage of us: for we are not ignorant of his devices.
2 Corinthians 2:11

MENTAL MOTIVATION

Bait comes when we're vulnerable and have unfulfilled voids, needs, and desires; such as: cognitive dissonance, loneliness, financial issues, troubled relationships, etc. Satan is a master at camouflaging what seem to be *reasonable solutions*. He is an *A+* student when it comes to studying us as his subjects, *'seeking whom he may devour.'*

There is nothing, NO-THING that takes God by surprise. Our situations are not new on this earth or in heaven. Solutions have already been provided. We should delay our actions until we receive the Word to move from God. Remember, a hungry fish reacting to floating bait, ends up on a human's plate. *Bait* is to destroy us. The *wait* is to develop us.

THOUGHTS TO ACTION…
- Identify the pain or issue that you are reacting to, but don't seek a quick fix.
- Do not underestimate your adversary.
- Meditate and speak specific scriptures pertaining to your situation.
- Keep the vision of a positive outcome before you and hold on to your faith.

40 Empowerment Thoughts

~12~

What you *meant* by your *intent* is not always what is *sent*.

The tongue of the wise commends knowledge, but the mouths of fools pour out folly
Proverbs 15:2

MENTAL MOTIVATION

The objective of effective communication is for the receiver and sender to exchange messages with full understanding of each other. When that doesn't happen, misunderstanding and offense may occur. It is a discipline to translate our thoughts into comprehensible words catered to the audience to whom we are speaking.

Have you ever made the statement to someone, *'I didn't mean it like that.'* Communicating does take work, but it doesn't have to be taxing. Learning and applying the knowledge of the personality and communication styles will empower people, enhance communication, and decrease the misunderstandings and offenses.
For information on personality styles go to www.mudworks.biz.

THOUGHTS TO ACTION…
- Think your intended message through.
- Acknowledge the weaknesses of your communication tendencies and make necessary adjustments.
- Take the primary responsibility for your message being understood.
- Identify the communication style of your audience and implement the skills to effectively get your message across.

~13~

Excuses are always available, but opportunities are not.

18 But they all with one accord began to make excuses. The first said to him, 'I have bought a piece of ground, and I must go and see it. I ask you to have me excused.' 19 And another said, 'I have bought five yoke of oxen, and I am going to test them. I ask you to have me excused.' 20 Still another said, 'I have married a wife, and therefore I cannot come.'
Luke 14:18-20

MENTAL MOTIVATION

Excuses are abuses to our future. Our future is cultivated or eliminated based on our choices made now. Cain tried to excuse himself as to why his offering was not acceptable (Genesis 4). Moses tried to excuse himself, as Israel's deliverer, because of a speech impediment (Exodus 4). Jesse tried to excuse David as the future king, because he was just a shepherd boy (1 Samuel 16). Do you make excuses when opportunities are presented?

Our potential *future self* is shouting at us, jumping up and down, waving the flag, hoping we make the right decision in the *now,* to fulfill our present opportunities. But the *present self,* if not disciplined, *can* rationalize, doubt, and find excuses to be removed from any further obligations of the opportunity. Do not give into excuses. Your *future self* depends on it.

THOUGHTS TO ACTION…
- ➢ Do not deny an opportunity, because you have not ironed out all details.
- ➢ Do not underestimate the God in you.
- ➢ God will put his *super* on your *natural,* resulting in supernatural achievements.
- ➢ Opportunities are not always going to look or be easy to master but know that you can do it. Just keep pursuing.

~14~

No one has your fingerprints; there are assignments only you can touch.

For we are his workmanship, created in Christ Jesus unto good works, which God hath before ordained that we should walk in them.
Ephesian 2:10

MENTAL MOTIVATION

You are a special agent; an ambassador sent on a special assignment to represent the One by whom you were sent. Imagine the theme song to MISSION IMPOSSIBLE playing while you're prepared to receive your special assignment. You are a member of the special task force to carry out the divine mission that only you can do.

There has never been anyone like you. Your fingerprints aren't shared by anyone on earth. You are the one chosen to unlock the doors of bondage to someone's cage, to usher the spiritually blind to the light, the voice of reason to the one who has lost his/her way. You were fearfully and wonderfully made (Psalms 139:14). You were destined to be a solution.

THOUGHTS TO ACTION...
- Celebrate your uniqueness.
- Identify the situations that you would like to fix.
- Be intentional in the impressions you make on others.
- Keep in mind, your touch can hurt or heal.

40 Empowerment Thoughts

> ~15~
>
> **When you know better and don't do better, you're no better.**

Therefore to him that knoweth to do good, and doeth it not, to him it is sin.
James 4:17

MENTAL MOTIVATION

This scripture is like a big wake-up slap! The scripture verse removes the weak excuse some use, *'God knows my heart.'* Most importantly, God know His Word. It is His Word by which we are judged and that He understands. When we have to use the excuse of, *God knows my heart,* it's a sign of intentional rebellion and justification of our actions or lack thereof.

King Saul in the fifteenth chapter of 1 Samuel was instructed to go into Amalek and destroy everything. King Saul decided to destroy everything except the king of the land and the 'best plunder' as a sacrificial offering to God. Saul knew what to do, but opted not to execute, which was a sin. His disobedience was the beginning of his demise. Know better and obey to achieve your best.

THOUGHTS TO ACTION...

- ➢ Do not minimize the effects of disobedience.
- ➢ Do not compromise the truth.
- ➢ Remember, we do not always get a second chance to do what should have been done the first time.
- ➢ Remember, God does not negotiate with good deeds in exchange for obedience.

~16~
Don't just stand for what is *Right*, stand for what is *Right*eous.

*He that followeth after righteousness
and mercy findeth life righteousness,
and honour.*
Proverbs 21:21

MENTAL MOTIVATION

Being *right* means you are in alignment with what is good, proper or in conformity with fact, reason, truth, or some standard. This is the type of person you want to be, living in the *right*. The main concern with being *right* is that it can be subjective to one's own interpretation and standards. Being in the *right* isn't a guarantee that others will always agree with your position of rightness.

Being *righteous* means you are acting in an upright and moral way according to God's standards. This kind of lifestyle supersedes any interpretation of what is right or wrong in man's eyes. Being *righteous* put you in right standing with God. In other words, it is all about Him. In today's society, a lot of things are accepted that are legally or socially *right* but are not *righteous*. Righteousness is even more unpopular than *right*. It brings about persecution, criticism, and more ostracizing. The important fact to remember is found in Matthew 10:28 (read it).

THOUGHTS TO ACTION...
➢ Don't compromise with the standards of man.
➢ Pray about the decision you make.
➢ Let biblical principles be your standard.
➢ Prioritize righteousness.

40 Empowerment Thoughts

> **~17~**
>
> **Invest moments with those you love to create experiences that last a lifetime.**

Wherefore comfort yourselves together, and edify one another, even as also ye do.
I Thessalonians 5:11

MENTAL MOTIVATION

There's a heartwarming Cheerios commercial of a father who works 3rd shift. He arrives home early morning after work at the time his wife and son are in the kitchen. The son is sitting at the table alone, eating cereal while looking up with sad eyes at his dad. In the next scene, the little boy gets up late at night and heads to the kitchen to get the box of Cheerios and milk. His dad walks in the kitchen, as he's preparing to leave for work and says, "Max, what are you doing up? It's late." His son looks up at his dad with puppy dog eyes and says, "I just wanted to have breakfast with you." The dad was so touched and sits to have a bowl of cereal with his son.

Devoting your time with the purpose to connect in relationships will reap a lasting and bountiful harvest. Unknowingly, people may develop behaviors, to compensate for voids created from lack of significant relationships. Cherish the moments.

THOUGHTS TO ACTION…
- ➢ Speak the Love Language of the person with whom you are connecting.
- ➢ Maximize moments spent; do not do it out of obligation.
- ➢ Seek to fulfill, not just fill voids.
- ➢ Find ways to affirm your loved ones.

40 Empowerment Thoughts

> ~18~
>
> **Jesus Christ is not Burger King**
> (have it your way),
> **He is the King of Kings**
> (it will be done His way)!

And he hath on his vesture and on his thigh a name written, KING OF KINGS, AND LORD OF LORDS.
Revelation 19:16

MENTAL MOTIVATION

We are guilty of treating Jesus as if he worked at a drive-thru restaurant; expecting to pull up to the menu board, give our order, and drive around to pick up our ordered blessing. It just doesn't work that way. The grace that is given to us and the many blessings we receive through our spiritual birthright are not a license to act as spiritual brats. God is moved by our reverence and faith. He is not moved by demands and self-centered expectations.

Referencing the story of Lazarus' death in John 11, Lazarus' family made Jesus aware of the severity of Lazarus' illness; yet he decided not to go to Lazarus at the time to heal him. Jesus decided to go after Lazarus died! To spectators, this made no sense. They felt Jesus was aware of his condition in enough time and could have gone to heal him before it was too late. But Jesus knew the ultimate plan of the Father, to demonstrate that HE is the Resurrection and Life and King of Kings!

THOUGHTS TO ACTION...
- Refrain from pride; it precedes failure.
- Do what touches the heart of God.
- Know that He is a God of His Word.
- Have faith that God knows best.

40 Empowerment Thoughts

> ~19~
>
> **Obedience brings breakthrough; disobedience brings breakdown.**

22 So Samuel said: "Has the Lord as great delight in burnt offerings and sacrifices, as in obeying the voice of the Lord? Behold, to obey is better than sacrifice, and to heed than the fat of rams. 23 For rebellion is as the sin of witchcraft..."
1 Samuel 15:22-23

MENTAL MOTIVATION

By nature, our flesh does not desire to be in compliance with anything that is opposite of what it wants and feels like doing. When sin entered into the world through disobedience of God's command, everything in it began to break down. Disobedience is sin, and sin puts a chasm between us and God. It leaves us disconnected from the Source that enables us to operate in our proper state.

Obedience is the bonding agent between us and God. Obedience stimulates an atmosphere of favor, protection, and abundance for our lives. When life's challenges come, a lifestyle of obedience can help provide the spiritual insurance policy needed to overcome life's challenges, versus the challenges overcoming us.

THOUGHTS TO ACTION…

- Examine the areas in your life that are challenging to your obedience.
- If you are not able to master your areas of struggle alone, get accountability!
- Do not second guess God's Word.
- Avoid conversations with those being used by Satan to subtly get you to compromise your obedience.

~20~

We do not exist for God to understand us; we exist to grow in the understanding of Him.

26He made from one man every nation of mankind to live on all the face of the earth, having determined their appointed times and the boundaries of their habitation, 27 that they would seek God, if perhaps they might grope for Him and find Him, though He is not far from each one of us;
Acts 17:26-27

MENTAL MOTIVATION

What an awesome revelation to know that the *when* and *where* we were born is intentional by God. As stated in the book of Acts, God desire for people to seek after Him, in order to understand the reason, He put us here. He is the Great I AM and always relevant in any age of time.

When we seek after God to get the revelation of Him, more of ourselves is revealed. God doesn't want to make the process difficult for us. Some ways to go about the process is to:
1. Pray about everything. 2. Pay attention to the pattern in which God communicates to you. 3. Have faith that God will reveal Himself.

THOUGHTS TO ACTIONS...
- Never believe that God is not relevant.
- Remember you did not create yourself.
- Study the Bible as the instructional manual for His creation.
- Actively pursue the heart of God; He's made provisions for you to get access to Him.

40 Empowerment Thoughts

~21~
Don't quit; otherwise, you will constantly be restarting.

And let us not be weary in well doing: for in due season we shall reap, if we faint not.
Galatians 6:9

MENTAL MOTIVATION

A *quitaholic* is one whom habitually finds excuses to avoid commitments and hinder all involved. Always looking for reasons why you are not competent or have the resources to fulfill a goal or obligation. So, where does this leave these types of people? It leaves them running in place and not moving forward; ending up with a *quitting* mentality.

Galatians 6:9 gives the promise of a harvest as long as we continue to push, press, and pursue in well doing. Here's another key in that scripture verse: *in due season!* That part of the verse is helping us understand that there is a higher administration that is orchestrating the timeframe appointed for the harvest to manifest to us. The harvest will only happen in that appointed time. If your harvest has not manifested, it is indicative that the current season isn't right and to keep going. No excuse, don't quit, you can do it.

THOUGHTS TO ACTION...
- Know, if God calls you, He'll back you.
- It's a faith walk; you must trust God.
- Don't underestimate your capacity.
- Don't quit; you are still responsible for it.

40 Empowerment Thoughts

~22~

A Champion's test has only one option:
A. Win
B. Win
C. Win
D. All of the Above

I press toward the mark for the prize of the high calling of God in Christ Jesus.
Philippians 3:14

MENTAL MOTIVATION

The word *champion* makes me think of Muhammad Ali. His mentality was that of an undefeated boxing champion and losing was not an option. His champion mentality was so contagious and inspiring to those who looked up to him. His ability to confidently express to his adversaries, that he was undefeated, usually caused some of them to second guess themselves.

This is the same kind of approach we must take in life. Mediocrity and complacency are culprits to a champion. A 'Champion' person exercises to build their physical muscles, mental muscles, and spiritual muscles. Exercising naturally and spiritually, keeps us in a prepared state to victoriously handle circumstances. Champions are undefeated thinkers.
YOU ARE A CHAMPION!

THOUGHTS TO ACTION…
- ➤ Master your crafts, skills, and abilities.
- ➤ Cultivate a winning mentality.
- ➤ Accept losses as steppingstones, not as defining moments.
- ➤ Because of your Creator, believe you were born a winner.

40 Empowerment Thoughts

~23~

Your spiritual growth doesn't happen by default. If it doesn't grow, It is your fault.

Wherefore, my beloved, as ye have always obeyed, not as in my presence only, but now much more in my absence, work out your own salvation with fear and trembling.
Philippians 2:12

MENTAL MOTIVATION

Anthony Robbins once said, "If you're not growing, you're dying." This profound statement is relevant to the spiritual aspect of our beings as well. Our spiritual growth will remain stagnant and decline if there is no intentional development on a consistent manner. The devil is counting on us not to do our spiritual work-out.

God's design of our spiritual nature requires a decision to grow. We are to seek after the Creator to understand the design of our creativity. If a lamp never plugs into the power source needed to give light, it does not fulfill the purpose it was created to do. We could accomplish many things and reach great heights in life, but if those accomplishments aren't accompanied by spiritual connectivity with God, there is no true gain.

THOUGHTS TO ACTION…
- You are a spiritual being; therefore, prioritize your spiritual growth.
- Memorize applicable scriptures.
- Practice a lifestyle of prayer.
- Connect to a biblically sound ministry to cultivate your spirit man.

~24~

A *"jack-ass"* brought deliverance in Balaam's life! Never underestimate or dismiss those who seem to give you a challenge.

³² And the angel of the LORD said unto him, Wherefore hast thou smitten thine ass these three times? Behold, I went out to withstand thee, because thy way is perverse before me: ³³ And the ass saw me, and turned from me these three times: unless she had turned from me, surely now also I had slain thee, and saved her alive.
Numbers 22:32-33

MENTAL MOTIVATION

I really believe God enjoys doing things out of our realm of the impossible in order to grab our attention, as He did with Balaam. He only allowed the donkey to see the angel at first, and then used the donkey to prevent Balaam from imminent destruction.

Balaam's ass (donkey) represents the people in our lives we ignore or get angered with, when they challenge or don't agree with us. These people may include our parents, spouses, children, friends, ministers, etc. Before being so quick to be offended and attack the person who might show resistance or lack of agreement with you; seek their heart of wisdom. God might be using them to get through to you.

THOUGHTS TO ACTION….

- ➤ Listen to other's insight regardless of their status.
- ➤ Listen for God's voice when you feel challenged.
- ➤ Do not be hasty to disregard opposing point of views.
- ➤ Don't mistreat someone if they disagree with your decision(s).

~25~
Don't let yourself be de-*SIN*-sitized to compromise.

And do not be conformed to this world, but be transformed by the renewing of your mind, that you may prove what is that good and acceptable and perfect will of God.
Romans 12:2

MENTAL MOTIVATION

In our world today any information is accessible with the click of a button or touch screen device. We are bombarded with so many opinions, theologies, facts, non-facts, social and entertainment media that make it challenging to diffuse amongst it all. If we aren't careful, we may find ourselves like the frog slowly boiling in a pot of water metaphor, and not realize it.

We have to be on guard, like never before, properly filtering the bombardment of information coming our way. We never want to be on the wrong side of the fence that calls evil good and good evil, just because of societal stances. Sin is sin, regardless of how it's packaged or decorated. Keep your eyes wide open for the devil's subtle devices; stay watchful.

THOUGHTS TO ACTION…
- Remember, God is always watching.
- Take a stand even if persecution follows.
- Know that the rewards are not always immediate, but they shall come to pass.
- Don't compromise for convenience.

~26~
Your intent must have intentional actions.

For the word of God is quick, and powerful, and sharper than any two-edged sword, piercing even to the dividing asunder of soul and spirit, and of the joints and marrow, and is a discerner of the thoughts and intents of the heart.
Hebrews 4:12

MENTAL MOTIVATION

The state of mind that directs one's actions towards something or someone defines the word *intent*. *Intentional* is the **on-purpose** aspect of the actions. Many times, I have had the mind/desire to get fit, but never align the actions to coincide with my intent. Or, I intended to do a better job in demonstrating to my loved ones how much I care, and I intended to accomplish long overdue goals, but with no intentional actions, nothing manifests. Not aligning our actions with intent can lead to an unfulfilled and frustrating life for us and those close to us.

Good intentions amount to nothing without purposeful execution. Les Brown states, "The graveyard is the richest places on earth." The graveyard is full of intents without intentional executed actions.

THOUGHTS TO ACTION...
- ➢ Align your actions with your intent.
- ➢ Don't make excuses for unexecuted intentions.
- ➢ Examine your thoughts to ensure your intents are good nature.
- ➢ Act how you want to be perceived.

40 Empowerment Thoughts

~27~

Don't hold on to a compliment as an excuse to be complicated.

Do nothing out of selfish ambition or vain conceit, but in humility consider others better than yourselves.
Philippians 2:3(NIV)

MENTAL MOTIVATION

It is one thing to be confident, but it's another thing to be a complicated individual. To clarify, do not excuse a characteristic or behavior that causes adverse effects, just because of prior expressions of admiration on that same characteristic or behavior.

For example, a person who is normally the life of the party, always cracking jokes, making people laugh, and appreciated by those in the atmosphere, will not see their behavior as an issue. Take this same characteristic/behavior in a more serious setting where the joking and laughter are a distraction and an irritation. If this individual holds onto prior compliments of the behavior, he will validate his actions. If he is unwilling to make appropriate adjustments to his behavior for the setting, he becomes a complication.

THOUGHTS TO ACTIONS…
- ➢ Be willing to adapt yourself; it doesn't change who you are.
- ➢ Seek objective feedback about yourself, along with affirmations.
- ➢ Respect the boundaries of others.
- ➢ Practice humility, a key to maintaining relationships.

40 Empowerment Thoughts

~28~

Choices you make consequences you take.

15And if it seems evil to you to serve the LORD, choose for yourselves this day whom you will serve, whether the gods which your fathers served that were on the other side of the river, or the gods of the Amorites, in whose land you dwell. But as for me and my house, we will serve the LORD."
Joshua 24:15

MENTAL MOTIVATION

Family Christian Center in Munster, IN puts on a phenomenal production called CHOICES. It shows how our choices will either lead us to Heartbreak Hotel or Hotel Hallelujah. But it all starts at the point where we're at the crossroads of selecting the options before us.

Consequences are simply the result of prior choices that were made. Not all choices are made by us; sometimes a choice is forced upon us. We have the ability to choose how we mentally and emotionally let forced choices affect us. Renowned minister, Joyce Meyers' story is an excellent example of overcoming forced choices from the past. Her choice to overcome has benefitted people around the globe. The consequences of our choices affect others as well.

THOUGHTS TO ACTION...
- ➢ Realize that your choices affect others.
- ➢ Take responsibility for consequences that occurred due to your choices.
- ➢ Do not expect others to accommodate if you make selfish choices.
- ➢ Think of others before deciding.

40 Empowerment Thoughts

~29~

You are an INFLUENCER, good or bad, you're INFLUENCING. How will you USE or abUSE your INFLUENCE?

13Ye are the salt of the earth: but if the salt have lost his savour, wherewith shall it be salted? It is thenceforth good for nothing, but to be cast out, and to be trodden under foot of men. 16Let your light so shine before men, that they may see your good works, and glorify your Father which is in heaven.
Matthew 5:13, 16

MENTAL MOTIVATION

Having the ability to affect the behavior, actions, and opinions of others is like an unrecognized **superpower**. At the same time, it is a huge responsibility to shoulder. The superpower of influence will have a lasting effect on anyone influenced by you. If you reflect on your own life, you will be able to recall those who have shaped your paradigms and helped to develop how you live life. Some of the influences have been intentional and some by default of circumstances.

We all have this **superpower** called influence. There are people you will meet in life whose lives will be built or damaged due to your ability to affect them. In becoming aware of your superpower, what will you do with it? Will your superpower be put to good use for the betterment of your family and society? Or will you allow the superpower of influence to, unintentionally happen. There are only two options as stated: properly *use* or ab*use*.

THOUGHTS TO ACTION…
- ➢ Do not use influence for selfish reasons.
- ➢ Be intentional with the use of your words around others.
- ➢ Continue to enhance yourself so that your influence will help better others.
- ➢ Aim for positive affect rather than a negative effect.

40 Empowerment Thoughts

~30~

The manifestation of your *vision* will enhance society.

₄₆ And Joseph went out from the presence of Pharaoh, and went throughout all the land of Egypt. ₄₇ Now in the seven plentiful years the ground brought forth abundantly.
Genesis 41:46-47

MENTAL MOTIVATION

- Peanut butter for a sandwich
- Lamps to illuminate a room
- A vehicle to transport from one location to another

The list could go on, but what is the significance of this list of gifts to our planet? They are all manifestations of someone's vision: George Washington Carver, Thomas Edison, Alessandro Volta, and Karl Benz. These are just a few who were willing to go forward in having their dreams materialize; the thought, that burning unction within them, was brought to life. They did not give up until their visions came to pass. As a result, they created foundations that generations could build upon and benefit. Society has issue(s) that the manifestation of your visions will solve.

THOUGHTS TO ACTION...

➢ Don't think an idea is too weird or crazy to pursue.
➢ Aim to pursue God's ideas vs. good ideas.
➢ Be willing to tread into unknown territory that others have not done.
➢ Despite obstacles, keep pursuing.

> ~31~
> ***Purging* must occur to accommodate *Purpose*.**

Purge me with hyssop, and I shall be clean: wash me, and I shall be whiter than snow.
Psalms 51:7

MENTAL MOTIVATION

When guests are scheduled to come to your home, you would normally go through the process of cleaning up to make things presentable for their arrival. The cleaning process will include both discarding and proper placement of things. Invited guests are usually people whom you desire to have visit, because they bring some form of pleasure or fulfillment to your life.

Purpose is like a guest we should desire to have permanently in our lives. But if Purpose does not have a place to sit due to the unnecessary life clutter, then the visitation will be delayed or possibly cancelled. Purging is the process of getting rid of whatever is impure or undesirable; to cleanse; to purify.

THOUGHTS TO ACTION...
- ➢ Determine what clutter is in your life.
- ➢ Let go of past issues and things that will not assist in your future.
- ➢ Do not ignore the lessons learned from the past.
- ➢ Practice daily maintenance of purging.

> ~32~
> **Do not let how others *act* cause you to *retract*.**

Blessed is the man who walks not in the counsel of the wicked, nor stands in the way of sinners, nor sits in the seat of scoffers
Psalms 1:1

MENTAL MOTIVATION

Have you ever cooked fried food at home and the whole house, including your clothing, becomes permeated with the smell? That is how it is when it comes to those you hang around. Their influential aroma affects you and your behavior. Sometimes the affect is subtle and you're unaware that your behavior is reflective and affected by those whom you hang around.

Whose aroma are you allowing to get on you? Retract means to *withdraw or to go back on (a promise or agreement)*. Your core values, religious beliefs, personal standards are the essence of you. Do not allow the negativity of others cause you to compromise and/or retract. We become a product of our influencers.

THOUGHTS TO ACTION...

➢ Examine who you are choosing to allow in your circle of influence.
➢ Examine your own personal belief system to make sure it is based on a firm foundation and truth.
➢ Associate with those who have the aroma you desire to have on you.
➢ Be willing to take a stand and feel comfortable in doing so.

40 Empowerment Thoughts

> **~33~**
> **Don't box your purpose in formalities; just build your purpose on THE FOUNDATION.**

And I say also unto thee, that thou art Peter, and upon this rock I will build my church; and the gates of hell shall not prevail against it.
Matthew 16:18

MENTAL MOTIVATION

Peter was a great example of a person who was not boxed into the way others operated. For example, Peter asked Jesus if he could step out of the boat and walk on water to him. Who in their natural mind would make such a request? Peter was a radical thinker and passionate about their mission. He didn't become a water-walker by letting man's boundaries influence him.

The Pharisees tried to box Jesus and his disciples into a trap called formalities of the laws and customs. But, Jesus, being **truth,** could not be bound by it. When you are not bound by the formalities of the ideologies of man, then you are at liberty to go forth in your unique purpose on a firm foundation. The foundation of truth will allow you to establish *produce* that will stand when non-foundational things will not.

THOUGHTS TO ACTION…
- ➤ Build your foundation on biblical principles.
- ➤ Do not allow others to dictate what you 'should do' in life.
- ➤ Seek counsel from unbiased mentors.
- ➤ Be true to yourself and honest with others.

40 Empowerment Thoughts

> ~34~
>
> **Don't let someone else's *perception*, based on their *reception*, be a *deception* that keeps you from obtaining your *possession*.**

I can do all things through Christ which strengthen me.
Philippians 4:13

MENTAL MOTIVATION

Be confident in the way you were naturally created. As stated before, we are shaped by our social circles, parents, educators, work environment, entertainment media, etc. But, in the timeline of birth to adulthood, if not carefully nurtured, we could succumb to spoken and unspoken expectations of what we 'should be' that could contradict 'who we truly are.'

If you have been a victim of an unhealthy growing environment or currently in non-nurturing relationships, do not allow the perception of yourself fall below that of how God sees you. He is the Creator and you are His creation. Within you is creativity to bring forth purposeful things of life. Don't let negative thinking from others or you sabotage or rob you of the fullness of your potential.

THOUGHTS TO ACTION…
- ➢ Do not practice a victim mentality.
- ➢ Cite a positive confession daily.
- ➢ Know your worth and value.
- ➢ Be free to be you.

~35~

10-1=9; 12x2-15=9; 3x3=9; 3+3+3=9: They all equal the same, just different methods of achieving the same result. One way over another is not best; it's all about which method is best for the situation.

Let us discern for ourselves what is right; let us learn together what is good.
Job 34:4

MENTAL MOTIVATION

A short description of the Four Personality Temperaments is as follows: Choleric (do it my way), Melancholy (do it the right way), Sanguine (do it the fun way), and Phlegmatic (do it the easy way). I won't go into depth on the Personality Temperaments, but for more information on the Personality Temperaments, go to www.mudworks.biz.

The various approaches may be viewed as: being too direct, taking too long to process details, being too playful, or being too slow. The key is to connect with the journey of a person whose process is different than yours. To maximize your personal and professional relationships, practice the discipline of the **Four A's**:

THOUGHTS TO ACTION...
- Acknowledge another's modus operandi.
- Accept that there is a different way of executing a plan.
- Add your contribution without negating another's process.
- Acquire the necessary skills to help you adapt to another's method.

~36~
To make the devil quit, to God, you must submit.

Submit yourselves therefore to God. Resist the devil, and he will flee from you.
James 4:7

MENTAL MOTIVATION

Propagating information as true when it's not is the devil's specialty trick with us. He works to sensationalize the need to give in to our fleshly desires and conveniences. The reason is to gain the necessary access to influence our will. The devil wants to take the wheel of our will! Being the vengeful and bitter being that he is, his sole desire is to steal, kill, and destroy (John 10:10) what belongs to God.

Once the devil gains access, as he did in the Garden, he then seeks to bully his way into other areas. He's like that unwelcomed guest who roams through your house without permission. Submission to God is the way to eradicate this pest from the bullying tactics. Submission is a taboo word to the human flesh, but if we want to see the enemy flee and let us be, we must submit (James 4:7).

THOUGHTS TO ACTION...
- ➢ Remember you can overcome.
- ➢ Yield your ways to God.
- ➢ Use scripture against the devil.
- ➢ Align your feelings and thoughts with Scripture.

~37~

God never compromises His standards to accommodate us! His grace and mercy are an extension, as a courtesy, for us to get up to HIS STANDARDS.

For if we sin wilfully after that we have received the knowledge of the truth, there remaineth no more sacrifice for sins…
Hebrews 10:26

MENTAL MOTIVATION

Imagine a universe of chaos where there is no order: a solar system not orbiting in a symphonic manner, the natural laws of physics operating in defiance and our biological makeup opts to not function as designed. This sounds like a universe without the standards of God. His standards are not to restrict us, but to protect us. If God compromised Himself, the universe would literally go into a chaotic state.

Fortunately, God does have a level of compassion towards His creation and He provides *mercy* [not giving what we do deserve] and *grace* [getting what we don't deserve]. We are not to take His compassion for granted and use it as a license to fall below standard. God truly loves us beyond our capacity to fully comprehend. God knows that people do not have the ability to meet the requirements. In His grace and mercy, He sent Jesus in our place to accommodate where we have fallen short.

THOUGHTS TO ACTION...
- ➢ Beware that intentional defiance will bring judgment.
- ➢ Align your core values with God's standards.
- ➢ Be grateful for God's grace and mercy.
- ➢ Rely on the Holy Spirit guidance.

40 Empowerment Thoughts

~38~

The *Pain*, that caused the *Stain*, will *Remain*, and prevent you from *Gain*, unless your relationship with Christ you *Maintain*, and let HIM fill you with the power to *Sustain*.

Surely God is my help; the Lord is the one who sustains me.
Psalm 54:4 (NIV)

MENTAL MOTIVATION

The suffering that one experiences in life, due to self-inflicted reasons, or the result of others, may be embedded in the heart and mind. The painful experiences have the potential of becoming festering blemishes that give a sense of dishonor and unworthiness. It will cause us to consciously or unconsciously develop insecurities and defense mechanisms to compensate for the shame of pain. Our lives begin to build around the pain and the dysfunction becomes normal.

In the scripture reference, Jesus is telling us that he will relieve us and provide us with a peace beyond our comprehension. When we accept the burden of pain as normal, we become oblivious to another way of life. To get from the *stain of pain* to *gain and sustain* will be a process you must go through in order to remove the ~**dys**~ from how you **function**. The best is available for us all.

THOUGHTS TO ACTION...
- ➤ Examine yourself for any unforgiveness.
- ➤ Forgive the offender and/or yourself.
- ➤ Get the necessary help in the process.
- ➤ Surrender the *stain of pain* to Jesus.

40 Empowerment Thoughts

> ~39~
>
> **The life you live affects the depth of favor for those associated with you.**

₁The LORD had said to Abram, "Go from your country, your people and your father's household to the land I will show you. ² "I will make you into a great nation, and I will bless you; I will make your name great, and you will be a blessing. ³ ... and all peoples on earth will be blessed through you.
Genesis 12:1-3

MENTAL MOTIVATION

God told Abram, "All peoples on earth will be blessed through you." Through one man, generation after generation has the access to experience the bestowal of divine favor, which we still experience today. This was the result of a common man with a heart for pleasing God.

Have you ever had your seat upgraded at an event, or received something extra because of whom you were associated? It is such an awesome treat to be the benefactor of the overflow of abundance because of your parents, or the church you attend, or friends you know. More importantly, strive to be the person that maintains good relations with God and man. Your loved ones can be blessed or cursed because of their association with you.

THOUGHTS TO ACTION...
- Prepare to take the consequences of the choice you make.
- *Avoid self-centered* decisions that have a negative effect on others.
- Execute *now* actions to positively affect your *later* generation.
- Live a life after the heart of God.

40 Empowerment Thoughts

~40~

Just because others FALL BACK, doesn't mean you can give the CALL BACK, God has for your life!

For the gifts and calling of God are irrevocable.
Romans 11:29 (NIV)

MENTAL MOTIVATION

Our lives are purposeful and unique. Acts 17:26-27, reminds us that God appointed the times and bounds for our existence; He intentionally crafted the blueprints for us and we must run our assigned race. The race will start off with many people throughout our lives: family, friends, spouses, children, co-workers, etc. Sometimes they will disappoint us, and we can become discouraged against continuing towards the goal of the high calling of God in Christ Jesus, but it's our race to run.

It was important for Jesus to remain focused on his Father God in order to continue fulfilling the assignment of the Cross. Those around him failed many times. They doubted him and themselves many times. They abandoned him when he needed them the most. But he looked up to the hills from where his help came from (Psalms 121:1) so that he wouldn't be discouraged by those around him and give up on the assignment he was sent to complete. We must follow in Jesus' example to accomplish our mission.

THOUGHTS TO ACTION...
- ➢ Remember God will never leave you.
- ➢ Take time to pray daily for strength.
- ➢ Always aim to please God as your first priority.
- ➢ Keep pressing on when others won't.

40 Empowerment Thoughts

MENTAL MOTIVATION

Your *Perspective*
determines
Your *Focus*

Your *Focus*
determines
Your *Approach*

Your *Approach*
determines
Your *Outcome*

Your *Outcome*
determines
Where You're Going

©Robert L. Watts, Jr.

40 Empowerment Thoughts

Personal Declaration...

Take a moment to reflect on what resonated in this book to you. Write down your own **THOUGHTS TO ACTON** that will propel you in the direction for which you were created.

_____
_____
_____
_____
_____
_____
_____
_____
_____
_____
_____
_____

For I know the thoughts that I think toward you, says the LORD, thoughts of peace and not of evil, to give you a future and a hope.
Jeremiah 29:11(NKJV)

MENTAL MOTIVATION

Prayer...

Dear God,

I thank You for the strength that You've given me to fulfill the intentions of Your Will. I am a unique craftsmanship created in Your love.

I will look to You for clarity, direction, and wisdom in every area of my life. May I live a life that is pleasing unto You so that I may obtain favor with You.

May my life be a blessing to those around me; be an encouragement for the discouraged; be a seed for those in need. Jesus be Lord over my life.

Amen!

40 Empowerment Thoughts

I am truly grateful that you have selected this book as one of your literary enlightenments. Please be sure to stay connected by following me on the following social media platforms so that you can be aware of other literary products and services offered. I hope that you will take any wisdom and spiritual nuggets obtained and implement them into your day-to-day life. May God bless you abundantly in all that you do according to His Will for your life. Remember to be intentional to live in purpose on purpose.

Be sure to join me on the following social medias:

Instagram: @drrob_
Twitter: @mentalmotive40
Facebook: Dr Rob Empowerment

Citation Notes…

Page 39
"Cheerios 3rd Shift Breakfast Commercial." *MarketMeNot*. N.p., n.d. Web. 29 Oct. 2014.
http://www.marketmenot.com/cheerios-3rd-shift-breakfast-commercial/

Chapman, Gary. *The 5 Love Languages*. Panama City. Norfield Publishing, 2010. Print.

Page 57
"Les Brown Quotes." Les Brown Quotes (Author of Live Your Dreams). N.p., n.d. Web. 04 Nov. 2014.
<http://www.goodreads.com/author/quotes/57803.Les_Brown>.

Page 75
Littauer, Marita Littauer and Littauer, Florence. *Wired That Way: The Comprehensive Personality Plan*. Grand Rapids: Revell, 2006. Print.

Watts, Natalie S. "Personalities." *Home Page*. N.p., May-June 2008. Web. 03 Nov. 2014.
http://www.mudworks.biz/home2.

40 Empowerment Thoughts

MENTAL MOTIVATION

Author's Ministry Organizations...

One Flesh Ministries was established in 2003 for the purpose of encouraging and networking with other married couples, enabling many opportunities of accountable in this marriage journey. Over the past years the ministry organization has evolved into providing services to not only marriages but also empowering the whole family dynamic. We host gatherings, events, workshops, and seminars to meet the needs of all aspects of the family unit.
www.onefleshministries.com

One Flesh Ministries Bible Institute (OFMBI) is to Biblically mentor, equip, and release those who are willing to accept the CHALLENGE of advancement and excellence in the Kingdom of God. OFMBI's goal is to provide a curriculum rooted in sound Biblical instruction for achieving advancement and excellence in ministry. OFMBI is a Satellite Teaching and Testing Center (STTC) of the Institute for Christian Works, headquartered in the state of South Carolina, from which all degrees and certificates are granted. OFMBI offers quality and affordable Christian educational programs through 100% Independent Study.

www.ofmbi.com

MENTAL MOTIVATION

40 Empowerment Thoughts

Additional Publications by
Younique Design, Inc.

www.youniquedesign.biz/menu

MENTAL MOTIVATION

Additional Recommended Resources...

Dr. Caroline Leaf is a world renowned Christian neuroscientist. For further information, go to: **www.drleaf.com**

40 Empowerment Thoughts

Best-selling author, Tony Robbins shares great insights in his book, Unleash The Power Within, to help the readers discover how to make life full of extraordinary success. For more information on Tony Robbins, go to:
www.tonyrobbins.com

MENTAL MOTIVATION

The late, Dr. Myles Munroe was truly one of the Kingdom generals of our time. He was known for being a man of great wisdom and a builder of leaders. For other products by Dr. Myles Munroe, go to:
www.munroeglobal.com

40 Empowerment Thoughts

Speak To Your Future by Dr. Steve Munsey will encourage readers to use unwavering faith for the promises of God in your life. For further information, go to:
www.stevemunsey.org

MENTAL MOTIVATION

www.ingramcontent.com/pod-product-compliance
Lightning Source LLC
LaVergne TN
LVHW021408080426
835508LV00020B/2503